ISBN 978-0-483-08811-5
PIBN 11296559

1 MONTH OF FREE READING

at

www.ForgottenBooks.com

By purchasing this book you are eligible for one month membership to ForgottenBooks.com, giving you unlimited access to our entire collection of over 1,000,000 titles via our web site and mobile apps.

To claim your free month visit:

www.forgottenbooks.com/free1296559

English
Français
Deutsche
Italiano
Español
Português

www.forgottenbooks.com

Mythology Photography **Fiction**
Fishing Christianity **Art** Cooking
Essays Buddhism Freemasonry
Medicine **Biology** Music **Ancient**
Egypt Evolution Carpentry Physics
Dance Geology **Mathematics** Fitness
Shakespeare **Folklore** Yoga Marketing
Confidence Immortality Biographies
Poetry **Psychology** Witchcraft
Electronics Chemistry History **Law**
Accounting **Philosophy** Anthropology
Alchemy Drama Quantum Mechanics
Atheism Sexual Health **Ancient History**
Entrepreneurship Languages Sport
Paleontology Needlework Islam
Metaphysics Investment Archaeology
Parenting Statistics Criminology
Motivational

GALENA
ILLINOIS

AN AMERICAN HERITAGE

Highlights of its History
GUIDE BOOK and MAP

ON SCENIC U. S. 20
The General U S Grant Highway

THE GREAT RIVER ROAD
the Scenic North-South highway

served by

ILLINOIS CENTRAL RAILROAD
GREYHOUND BUS LINES

———————◆———————

AIR CONDITIONED or AIR COOLED ROOMS

THE **DE SOTO HOUSE** has maintained more than a century of
continuous hospitality It was the center of activities and festivities during
the Civil War era **TODAY** offers you a choice of 60 guest rooms, from
modest to the finest! TV and free parking

CENTRALLY LOCATED

———————◆———————

GALENA—The Ideal Spot for Conventions, Vacation and weekends
Tourist Information and Convention Bureau
Write to —De Soto House, Galena, Illinois

———————◆———————

MANITOUMI LAND – "THE LAND OF GOD"

GALENA was a lusty roaring boom-border river port, and a supply depot for the Northwest territory, when Chicago was little more than a crossroad.

THE INDIANS believed that "Manitou"—the Great Spirit—dwelled in this hilly paradise nestled between the Rock, Mississippi and Wisconsin Rivers.

LEAD, FUR, AND THE RIVER brought the earliest white settlers, and by 1830 the area population was close to 10,000. River traffic increased steadily until the late 1850's with commercial steamers and regular packet service operating from Galena south to St. Louis and north to St. Paul.

GALENA'S MARKETS via this water route were far flung,—thru New Orleans to the eastern seaboard and thence on to European ports. Between 1850 and 1860 Galena was the lead mining capital of the country and the commercial capital of the Upper Mississippi River Valley.

THE RAILROADS which brought growth and greatness to Chicago, sealed the doom of Galena's commercial dominance. Traffic on the river route declined as trade of the interior states was shipped overland to the seaboard via rail, military roads, and subsequently by highways.

THIS CHANGE in the pattern of trade routes in the decade preceding 1860, gradually severed the economic cord which previously had bound the upper Mississippi Valley states to the southern states.

IN RETROSPECT we can see how this east-west ribbon of rail brought the northern states closer together in economic dependence, and THEREBY STRENGTHENED SUPPORT OF THE UNION DURING THE CIVIL WAR YEARS.

LEAD WAS THE MAGNET THAT BROUGHT
THE FIRST SETTLERS

THE PRESENCE OF LEAD ORE in the upper Mississippi Valley (now parts of Iowa, Wisconsin and Illinois) was reported by French explorers as early as 1658. This was the first major lead-producing section in the United States

THE PROMISE OF WEALTH brought men from all directions to claw at the earth's surface in the hope of striking "pay dirt."

THE MISSISSIPPI BUBBLE

The Galena mine area was included in that famous wildcat promotion scheme launched in 1717, when glowing tales of the rich mineral fields of the upper Mississippi Valley reached John Law, Scotch adventurer in Paris, France Fraudulently claiming that this rich mineral area was under development by his "Company of the West" his stocks pyramided, then collapsed, and the "Mississippi Bubble" was broken.

ILLINOIS—THE "SUCKER" STATE

Many of the early Fever River prospectors traveled overland in covered wagons; others came by keelboat. Some brought their families and only enough supplies for the summer months. These southerners could not stand the severe Illinois winters, so they worked the mines in the summer and fall, returning to their homes before winter set in.

They were dubbed "Suckers" after the migratory fish that seasonally traveled up and down the mighty Mississippi. From this origin Illinois is still called the "Sucker" state; Illinoisans are referred to as "Suckers".

"GALENA" IS BORN!

Mining proved so lucrative that by 1826 not only miners but farmers, merchants, mechanics, and professional men were arriving in Galena in large numbers. Often a farmer following his plow would hear the rumble caused by a miner's blast deep below his furrow.

It was December 27, 1826, when the mining settlement known as "LaPointe" kicked off its swaddling clothes and became a town named "Galena". A town which within a year mushroomed into a hundred and fifteen houses and stores.

* * *

THE FEDERAL GOVERNMENT granted leases to early miners, calling for a ten percent royalty on the lead produced; later the rate was reduced to six percent. However, collecting the royalty was not successful, and the Government decided, in 1847, to sell the lands outright.

By the 1850's mining became costlier as the shallow diggings were worked out, and expensive machinery became necessary for depth mining.

LEAD AND ZINC are currently being mined in this area, by Eagle-Picher Company and by Tri-State Zinc Inc.

Illinois Central Engine at Galena, beside the scale used to weigh pig lead— when Galena area supplied more than 80 percent of this country's lead output.

STEAMBOAT ROUND THE BEND!

SIDNEY—Sternwheel packet and excursion paddleboat. Wood hull 221.3' x 35.5', engines 17's, 5½' stroke, four boilers.

Sounds of the calliope and strains of sweet music from the band wafted on the breeze when sidewheeler and sternwheel paddleboats appeared as beautiful swan-like visions floating regally on the water with paddlewheels churning a misty spray.

Steamers pulled into the Galena levee with banners streaming, flags flying and bands playing—amid the huzzas of the passengers and those lined at the shore. On special occasions the cannon of the city guards thundered its throaty welcome.

ULYSSES S. GRANT was thirty-eight years old when he moved to Galena —in 1860—arriving with his wife and their four small children, aboard the "Itasca".

ITASCA Sidewheel packet, wood hull (1857-1868), 230' x 35', Engines 22's, 7-ft. stroke, 4 boilers, 560 tons. Paddlewheels 28' diameter, 10' buckets.

THE "IRON HORSE"
CHANGED THE TIDE OF TRAVEL AND COMMERCE

The Illinois Central's No. 1

Thousands of people came to Galena, "The First American Klondike", by conestoga wagon, buckboard, on horseback, by foot, and by steamboat. They came from all parts of this country and from European countries.

In 1825 Oliver Kellogg broke a wagon trail from Peoria to Dixon and on to Galena, but travel was slow, hazardous and seasonal.

The year of 1850 marked the real beginning of the railway era in Illinois *The Illinois Central* launched a widespread publicity campaign, drawing attention to climate, resources and opportunity in this then "far west" country.

ADVERTISEMENTS carrying illustrations of farm crops, cattle grazing on fertile prairies, scenes of peace and plenty, beckoned hardy sons of toil to Illinois, *"The Garden of America"*.

Later the Illinois Central Railroad sold land to these settlers at $1.25 per acre. Purchase could be made at 50c down payment per acre, with seven years in which to pay the remainder. Holders of government script could purchase land for 62½c per acre.

BUILDING A PIONEER RAILROAD was a formidable undertaking. The work was done by men of brawn and courage, with shovels, picks, crow bars and sledge hammers. Hundreds of oxteams and horse-teams were required to transport materials and supplies.
As many as ten thousand workmen were employed at one time on different sections of track.

AT 4½ P. M. ON NOVEMBER 8, 1854, A THIRTEEN-GUN SALUTE ANNOUNCED ARRIVAL OF THE ILLINOIS CENTRAL TRAIN IN GALENA, CARRYING DIGNITARIES AND OUT-OF-TOWN GUESTS WHO CAME HERE TO CELEBRATE COMPLETION OF THE IRON RAILS LINKING GALENA WITH CHICAGO AND THE EAST COAST.

A PROCESSION FORMED AT THE RAILROAD DEPOT THEN MARCHED TO THE DESOTO HOUSE WHERE THE BANQUET WAS HELD IN THE 300-SEAT DINING ROOM.

HARDY PIONEERS TRANSFORMED ILLINOIS from a desolate prairie. Houses, schools and churches were erected near the little wooden railroad stations, and streets were platted.

THE "CIVILIZING RAILS" brought people from every walk of life. Settlements mushroomed into towns, and *between 1850 and 1860 "the population of Illinois more than doubled."*

DEPENDABLE YEAR-AROUND RAIL SERVICE by all railroads aided agricultural and industrial expansion and contributed to the prosperity and growth of the United States.

ILLINOIS CENTRAL ENGINE 1380; an American-type locomotive, with a 4-4-0 wheel arrangement.

Illustrations Courtesy Illinois State Historical Library

View of Galena during the romantic era when all upper Mississippi River traffic registered cargo at the U. S. Customs office here.

GALENA — County seat of Jo Daviess County. Cradled in majestic hills "The Town That Time Forgot" is a living picture of a fabulous era in the midwest's great historic past. **NATIONALLY KNOWN.**

PICK AND SHOVEL DAYS AT THE KIPP MINE
Mineral was brought to the surface in wooden tubs, where it was washed to separate the mineral from the dirt.

GRANT HOME STATE MEMORIAL
Pickford El Morning Star Photo

THE 18TH PRESIDENT OF THE UNITED STATES LIVED HERE! April 27, 1957 Governor William G Stratton dedicated the 12-room Victorian house, which was restored by the Illinois Department of Conservation The occasion was the Third Annual U S Grant Pilgrimage, 900 Boy Scouts and Explorers participated in the dedication ceremonies.

GALENA HISTORICAL MUSEUM

A TREASURE HOUSE OF EARLY AMERICANA! Outstanding among the more than 6,500 items, is the Thomas Nast life-size oil painting "Peace In Union."

A "Civil War Room" places special emphasis on participation by residents of Jo Daviess County.

AN ARCHITECTURAL GEM

Hon E B. Washburne was Secretary of State under President U S. Grant Later he was U. S Ambassador to the Court of France.

E. B. WASHBURNE HOME

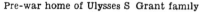

Pre-war home of Ulysses S Grant family

From this home "Captain" U. S Grant answered President Abraham Lincoln's call for 75,000 men to save the Union

THE MAGIC CARPET !

YOU WILL LONG REMEMBER GALENA! It is mellow with the tones which only the Master Painter can create; and situated in a scenic region the Indians called Manitoumi Land, the "Land of God".

The rich mineral resources lured men, and in the 1820's several thousands came here, making it the richest town in the State. The fabulous paddleboat era swept the town into its "Golden Decade of the Forties" as the most important commercial point on the upper Mississippi River north of St. Louis.

Galena is fascinating! It defies the description of Illinois as a "Prairie State". Nestling in the hills, it is surrounded by unsurpassed natural beauty, and within the town architectural treasures clinging to the hillsides - combined with its rich historic treasures - create an Old World charm.

In this shrine-dotted town you will be awakened to a new kinship with early pioneers and a deep feeling of awe. At the leisurely pace of yesteryear it will inspire you and give you a deep feeling of reverence.

This American Heritage recalls a way of life more than a century ago, and a deep appreciation of the struggles of pioneers clearing the land, building homes in the architecture of their old world homelands. It will turn your thoughts to the romance, the adventure, and the culture of that era, when they mined for lead, engaged in riverboat commerce, built roads, and by their dreams and their efforts left their imprint in the development of this great nation.

These were the men and women that played an important part in the Civil War. Galena and this area contributed many great personalities to the Union, and it later was from here that "Captain" Ulysses S. Grant left in 1861, later to become the greatest Northern General.

This too was the town from which U. S. Grant left in 1869 to take office as 18th President of the United States.

Galena citizens are humbly proud of their heritage, and God-given natural resources and scenic terrain. They are aware of the physical reminders here today for the teaching of visual history of our American ideals.

> History walks with you, as monuments to an illustrious past break through at every turn. Here you will see original landmarks lived in by pioneers. Architectural treasures, quaint nineteenth century charm and an air of tranquility, are a pleasant relief from today's fast tempo of living.
>
> !

THE ROAD TO ADVENTURE

leads to

GALENA !

Hospitable hotels and motels offer a selection of accommodations; restaurants offer a variety of menus! Antique stores invite the antique-seeker! A novel shopping center on quaint Main Street mingles with scenic and historic points of interest.

YEAR AROUND RECREATIONAL FACILITIES - Three parks, a swimming pool, outdoor roller skating rink, daily fee golf course and bowling alley. Game and pan fish. Fine hunting, including duck and deer hunting. View the shoreline of the mighty Mississippi, from the deck of an excursion boat Marine harbor now being developed. Camping facilities, and picnicking locales nearby.

CHESTNUT HILLS - winter ski area and summer recreational facilities, nine miles from Galena.

GALENA, located in the northwestern corner of Illinois, is centrally located for many circular drives in nearby Iowa and Wisconsin as well as in Illinois. For instance, Crystal Lake Cave in Dubuque, Iowa, The Grotto at Dickeyville, or Nelson Dewey Home and Park at Cassville, Wisconsin. Or continue your drive to Prairie du Chien, and return to Galena on the Iowa side of the Mississippi River. Apple River Canyon State Park, the Mississippi Palisades are just a short, but scenic, drive from here.

YOU WILL ENJOY YOUR STAY IN GALENA! Bring the family, and your camera or palette! For special Galena events, check the Calendar of Events in the back of this book.

PEACE IN UNION
LIFE-SIZE OIL PAINTING IN GALENA MUSEUM

It was presented to the City of Galena by H H Kohlsaat at the 1895 Grant Birthday ceremonies The artist, Thomas Nast of Civil War fame, was present Illustration, courtesy Illinois State Library.

A. E-2 U. S. 20 BRIDGE   Main St.
GALENA - a boom river town when Chicago was a
swamp. The now-narrowed Galena River was once
more than 340 feet wide, and upon its crest float-
ed palatial steamers and heavily loaded packets.

B. D-2 THE LEVEE   was the pulse of Galena;
the river was its route to and from its far-flung
markets. As many as eighteen steamers were tied
up at one time loading or unloading at the levee.

C. C-2 LOUISVILLE HOUSE   601 S.Main
Privately owned. Built in the 1820's as an hotel
for river and stagecoach travellers.

D. C-2 THE FLOOD GATES can be closed in event
of flood. The Galena River has at times given
forceful reminders of its turbulent past.

CENTURY OLD BUILDINGS frame Galena's bow-shaped
Main Street - mute testimony to her once booming
industries in the days when all upper Mississippi
River traffic registered in the U. S. Customs
Office here.

E. C-2 FLOOD PROTECTION DIKE The dike and the
20-foot high gates at the south entrance to this
town, protect the business district from flood.

F. C-2 OLD GRAIN HOUSES   The four 4- story
buildings on the West side of Main Street in the
500 block. Heavily loaded wagons once lined Bench
Street, waiting to be unloaded. Grain was dropped
from the 3rd floor Bench Street entrance to the
Main Street level of these warehouses.   Then the
grain was sacked and loaded on barges bound for
distant markets.

G. C-2 COMMISSION HOUSE   420 S. Main
Here waterfront business was transacted when
Galena's warehouses were a market well worth
cultivating.

GALENA of 1858 was a metropolis of the northwest.
It supported two daily newspapers, and a dozen
mills were operated here. Lumber yards, brick
and lime kilns, seven breweries, pottery shops,

three soap and candle factories, wagon shops, and three leather finishing houses, were doing a "land office" business.

1. C-2 DESOTO HOUSE corner Main and Green Sts.
In April 1855 the 240 room DeSoto House, with accommodations for four hundred guests, opened as the "largest hotel in the West". Six to seven hundred persons were arriving daily by riverboat, stagecoach and railroad, and rooms in this magnificient House were in great demand.

Abraham Lincoln spoke from the now-removed balcony in 1856. Ulysses S.Grant maintained his 1868 presidential headquarters here. The DeSoto House was the scene of many resplendent military cotillions during the Civil War era.

These original walls have echoed to stirring debates of national trends, inspired by voices of the wise and learned leaders in culture, music, art, philosophy and statesmanship.

As Galena's population and prestige declined, there was no longer need for such a large hostelry. In 1880 the two upper stories, closed since 1875, were removed. The seventy remaining rooms are now individually appointed for the modern comforts of today's travellers.

2. C-2 U. S. POST OFFICE Green St.
Constructed as a Customs House in 1858, for use of the river traffic. Erected under the direction of Ely S. Parker, a full-blooded educated Indian of the Seneca Tribe. He was Brigadier General and Military Secretary for General U. S. Grant.

3. C-2 THE GENERAL STORE S. Main
A facinating, well-stocked reconstructed General Store, Office, Bar Room and Kitchen.

4. C-2 GALENA GAZETTE & ADVERTISER 222 S. Main
Founded 1834; second oldest newspaper in Illinois.

5. C-3 GRANT LEATHER STORE 211 S. Main
A reconstructed Leather Store of the 1860's.

6. C-2 FRINK-WALKER STAGE LINE 212 S.Main
Site of the Stage Depot, Hall and Tavern. Frink-
Walker sent the first stagecoach from Galena to
Chicago in 1836. By 1857 fifteen stage lines
radiated from this town.

7. C-2 Site of J.R.GRANT STORE 120 S. Main
See D.A.R. placque. It was here that Ulysses S.
Grant worked for his father, from the spring of
1860 to the spring of 1861.

8. B-3 THE CRACK POT ANTIQUES 116 S. Main

9. B-3 OLD MARKET HOUSE Commerce & Perry.
Opened June 27, 1846. This Greek Revival struc-
ture is the oldest Market House in the Midwest. A
State Memorial; free admission.

10. B-3 MARKET SQUARE
Matrons in hoopskirts and shawls mingled on the
square with heavily-clad farmers, rough looking
miners in ocher-stained flannel shirts and heavy
leather boots, and Indians in colorful blankets.

For a daily fee of 25¢ a farmer could park on the
square and sell his farm produce direct from his
wagon to the bustling crowd. The latest gossip
and heated discussions of current topics, could
always be heard "on the square".

11. B-3 THE LAST COBBLESTONE STREET
Perry Street between Main & Bench Streets .

12. B-3 AMOS FARRAR CABIN 208 Perry
Open to the public. The present house is built
around the log cabin which stood inside THE OLD
STOCKADE. During the Indian uprising it was a
shelter for women and children. See D.A.R.placque.

13. B-3 FIRST POST OFFICE 200 N. Main
Now Robertson's Drug Store. On June 4, 1826 the
first post office in Galena was located on this
site; known as the "Fever River" post office.

14. B-3 2nd COUNTY COURTHOUSE 216 N. Main
Erected 1836. Now J. P. Vincent & Sons Monument
Works. Half of this building was rented to the

County for use as a courthouse. It held the first
theater of the lead mining area, in 1838, when
the Jefferson-McKenzie Players came from Chicago
in open wagons to play in Galena.

15. B-3 DOWLING'S STONE STORE Diagonal St.
Erected 1826; the oldest stone structure remaining in Galena. In its day of log cabins it was
unique due to its heavy walls of native stone.

16. B-3 DOWLING SHOP ANTIQUES Diagonal St.

17. A-4 OLD TOWN Broadway Ave.
See the old street lights, small parkway in the
center of the street, framing the old and quaint
buildings. This was the original site of the city.
In the early days a cooper shop, a tannery,a saw-
mill and a smelter operated here. Expansion of
industries caused building of the business section
in its present location.

18. B-4 PEDESTRIAN BRIDGE across Galena River
Located at the site of the 1847 Meeker Street
Toll Draw-Bridge.

19. A-4 SWIMMING POOL
Located two blocks north of the Pedestrian Bridge,
on the Scales Mound Road. At the site of the old
Fair Grounds.

20. A-3 JO DAVIESS COUNTY COURT HOUSE
Erected 1839 312 N. Bench
Captain U. S. Grant offered his West Point train-
ing and Mexican War experience at a mass meeting
held here in April 1861, when President Abraham
Lincoln called for 75,000 volunteers to save the
Union.

21. A-3 ST.MARY'S CATHOLIC CHURCH 400 Franklin.
Founded 1850. In 1856 the first brick edifice was
erected following plans by Father Samuel Charles
Mazzuchelli, O. P.

22. B-3 TAYLOR HOUSE ANTIQUES 201 N. Bench
Special Christmas Room! Victorian Room! Eagles
Roost! Party Paper Room! Village Store! and
the Littlest Import Shop!

23. B-2 DOWLING HOUSE   120 N.Bench
A storybook house;erected 1847. Privately owned.
Parts of this house were used as description for
the home of fictional Abby Delight, the heroine
of Janet Ayer Fairbanks' popular novel of 1932-
"The Bright Land."

24. B-2 FIRST PRESBYTERIAN CHURCH 108 N.Bench
Founded 1828.   Erected 1838.   The oldest Presbyterian Church in Illinois in continuous use. The
"Guild" of this church sponsors the Annual Pilgrimage through Historic Homes,

25. B-2 GALENA FIRE STATION   101 S.Bench
The city is speedily and efficiently protected
by our Volunteer Fire Department.

26. B-2 GRACE EPISCOPAL CHURCH 109 S. Prospect.
Founded 1827. Erected 1847. A grey stone, vine
covered edifice, buttressed and castellated in
Tudor style. Stained glass windows imported from
Belgium; magnificient alter, reredos and choir
stalls of hand carved black walnut. The delicate
silvery tones of the 1838 one-manual organ have
been strengthened by an alectric blower.

27. A-2 BLACK HAWK WAR MEMORIAL   S. Prospect
In 1832 Galena became a fortified military camp.
A runway was built from this military out-
look post to the Amos Farrar cabin inside the old
stockade. Bouldar marker placed by the D.A.R.

28. A-2 DR. EDW. KITTOE HOME   105 High
He was surgeon & Medical Director of the Army of
Tennessee; a Lieut. Col. on Grant's staff.

29. A-1 GEN. JOHN A. RAWLIN'S HOME   517 Hill
He was Chief of Grant's war staff; and Secretary
of War during Grant's presidency.

30. A-1 GEN. WM. R. ROWLEY HOME   515 Hill
Clerk of the Circuit Court. A Brigadier   General
& Provost Marshal on Grant's staff.

31.   VILLAGE BARN & LITTLE ACRES
(not shown on map.   Highway 20-W at Division
Location of "Country Fair" on specified dates.

32. A-1 1812 CEMETERY   Washington & Dodge
In this pioneer cemetery are the graves of many
first settlers.

33. B-1 GRANT'S PRE-WAR HOME   121 High
D.A.R. placqued. Captain Grant left from this
home in 1861. to enter the Federal Army.

34. B-1 ST. MATTHEW'S LUTHERAN CHURCH 127 High
Organized September 22, 1858.

35. C-1 A SCENIC VIEW The plaza in front of
the Central Elementary School is a vantage point
from which to view the valley and hills beyond.

36. C-1 WHITE HOUSE ANTIQUES 413 S. Prospect
In 1833 Dan Wann contracted for construction of
this house. Instead of cash, payment was stipu -
lated as "..lead delivered at the Galena wharf".

37. C-1 THE SCHOOL STEPS   Green St.
Numerous such stairways carry pedestrians .

38. B-2 QUALITY HILL   S. Prospect
The roaring life of the mines and river trade
brought wealth, and "Quality Hill" grew, blending
a new way of living with an Old World nostalgia.

39. C-1 METHODIST MANSE   S. Prospect
Privately owned. This former Methodist manse
was the home of Bishop Vincent, founder of the
National Chatauqua.

40. B-2 FELT'S FOLLY   125 S. Prospect
Privately owned. Victorian mansion, built in the
1840's by Lucius Felt. The stone steps, costing
$40,000, were dubbed "Felt's Folly".

The house has a ballroom in the mansard. It con-
tains 23 rooms including seven bedrooms with
original marble washstands. A pretentious home
with beautiful landscaped gardens.

OUR SPIRITUAL HERITAGE

FIRST METHODIST CHURCH
Founded 1829
Spiritual home of the Ulysses S. Grant
family. Their pew is appropriately placqued.
125 S. Bench Street   (Map No. 42 B-2)

FIRST PRESBYTERIAN CHURCH
Founded 1828   Erected 1838
108 N. Bench St.   (Map No. 24 B-2)

GRACE EPISCOPAL CHURCH
Founded 1827   Erected 1847
109 S. Prospect St.   (Map No. 26 B-2)

THESE MORE-THAN-CENTURY-OLD CHURCHES
INVITE YOU TO WORSHIP WITH THEM

**HILL PRESBYTERIAN
CHURCH**
West St. near Washington St.
(Located beyond the limits of
the attached map)

SOUTH PRESBYTERIAN CHURCH
Founded January 5, 1846   Erected **1847**
513 South Bench Street   (Map No. 51 D-1)

In September 1960 the South Presbyterian Church
and the Hill Presbyterian church united, and now are
known as the WESTMINSTER UNITED PRESBY-
TERIAN CHURCH.

ST. MARY'S CATHOLIC CHURCH
Founded 1850
400 Franklin Street   (Map No. 42 A-3)

ST. MICHAEL'S CATHOLIC CHURCH
Founded 1832   217 S. Bench Street
(Map No. 47 C-2)

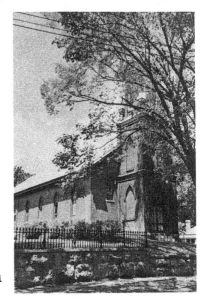

ST. MATTHEW'S EVANGELICAL
LUTHERAN CHURCH
127 High Street   Map No. 34 B-1

 For new vistas in a variety vacationland,
THE GREAT RIVER ROAD

Along this 573-mile scenic corridor are numerous State Parks and Memorials, photo-scenic lookout spots offering magnificent panoramic views, Indian Mounds, historic and architectural treasures.

Sportsminded travelers will find good hunting and fishing, harbor and boat launching facilities and waterfront recreation, a variety of nature trails, picnic and camping sites. Numerous spring and fall festivals are held in towns along this route.

Nineteen hundred pilot wheel markers, from East Dubuque to Cairo, will guide motorists. On the 1961 official Illinois Highway Department maps, the route of the GREAT RIVER ROAD is identified with miniature reproductions of the markers.

41. B-2   TURNER HALL   103 S. Bench
Has many historic associations. Though gutted by
fire and remodeled since it was built in 1874,
this auditorium with its double-decked boxes beside the stage, recalls the hey-dey of the Victorian stage.

42. B-2   FIRST METHODIST CHURCH   125 S. Bench
Founded 1829.   Spiritual home of the U. S. Grant
family. Their pew is appropriately   placqued.

43. C-2   WASHINGTON ST. STEPS   S. Bench
The path taken by U. S. Grant from his home   on
High Street, to the J.R.Grant Store on Main St.

44. C-2   FIRE HOUSE No. 1   S. Bench
Six such small structures housed the hand- drawn
equipment, so that apparatus would not have to be
drawn long distances.

Inside, can be seen a hand-drawn and manually
operated 1855 pumper used by our volunteer fire-
men. In the bell tower hangs the last old   fire
bell in Galena. The Galena Volunteer Fire   Company was organized February 1, 1830.

45. C-2   HISTORICAL MUSEUM   211 S. Bench
This building houses the City Hall, Community
Hall and the Museum. Outstanding among the more
than 6500 items of early Americana and the Civil
War era, is the life-size oil painting   "Peace
in Union" depicting Lee's surrender to Grant at
Appomatox.

46. C-2   CROSS THE STREET
See the row of brick houses recreating an   Old
World Atmosphere. Here the Bench street entrance
to Main Street buildings, is by narrow bridges
from the sidewalk to the houses.

47. C-2   ST. MICHAEL'S CHURCH   217 S. Bench
The "cradle of Catholicity" in the Northwest.
This was a flourishing parish before the first
Catholic church was founded in Chicago. Father
Samuel Charles Mazzuchelli, O. P., was its most
renouned Pastor.

48. C-2 THE NEWHALL HOME 235 S. Bench
Erected 1847 by Dr. Horatio Newhall, a pioneer
physician. Verandas were added in the 1890s.
A massive structure, topped by an octagonal
cupola. Now, the Nash Funeral Home .

49. C-2 CHURCH OF THE NAZARENE 301 S. Bench
Organized September 10, 1944.

50. B-1 ST. MICHAEL'S PAROCHIAL SCHOOL
Since 1880. 413 S. Bench

51. D-1 SOUTH PRESBYTERIAN CHURCH 513 S. Bench
Founded Jan. 5, 1846. Erected 1847. Members of
this church sponsor the Violet Show and Old South
Activities annually held on "Tour Weekend".

52. D-1 FELT CARNEGIE LIBRARY 601 S. Bench
Organized 1835. Building erected 1908.

53. D-1 FREDERICK STAHL HOME 603 S. Bench
Erected 1834. Privately owned. He took the first
load of lead from here to Chicago in 1833, at the
time the Potawattomie Treaty was made. He loaded
the wagons, drawn by two eight-oxen teams, with
3500 pounds of lead each, and travelled via Dixon.

54. D-1 THE OLD STORE - ANTIQUES 334 Spring

55. E-1 JOHN E. SMITH HOME 807 S. Bench
Erected in the 1850's. He operated a jewelry and
silversmith store in Galena at the start of the
Civil War. A Major-General on Grant's staff.

✳✳✳✳ ✳✳✳✳

ON THE EAST SIDE

56. E-3 E. B. WASHBURNE HOME 908 Third
Privately owned. Built in 1833; remodeled and en-
larged in the 1850's. On the lawn of this Southern Colonial residence Grant drilled the first
raw recruits from this area in '61. E.B.Washburne
served eighteen years in Congress. He was U.S.
Ambassador to the Court of France during Grant's
administration.

57. E-3   ILLINOIS CENTRAL RAILROAD DEPOT
                        Foot of Bouthillier St.
In 1854 the "Iron Horse" of the "Central" railroad roared across the prairie into this metrop -
olis of the midwest. General Grant alighted   at
the Illinois Central Station August 18, 1865. He
departed from here to take office as 18th president of the United States.

58. D-3   GRANT PARK   Park Ave at Jackson St.
Dedicated in 1891,when the first U.S.Grant Cele-
bration was held. See the bronze memorial statue
"Grant - our Citizen". The Fountain was present-
ed to the city by the G.A.R. Ladies Auxiliary .
Canons can be seen here from the Civil War,   the
Spanish American War, and World War I .

59 D-3   PANORAMIC VIEW   A favorite spot
for artists and camera enthusiasts.   Looking
westward the beauty of the town stands out as in
a mural.

60. D-4   CAPT. ORRIN SMITH HOME
                   S.E. Corner Jackson & Park Av.
He was a wealthy, colorful and pious boatman.
Where ever his boat might be at midnight Saturday
night, she was tied up, and not moved again until after midnight Sunday night. If no   minister
was available Cap't Smith led religious service .

61. C-4   THE ROCK HOUSE ANTIQUES   Third St.

62. C-4   THE UNION HOUSE   403 Park Av.
When built in 1839, this was a tavern accommoda -
ting four boarders. A stairway led from   the
rear porch to the river below.

63. D-4   GRANT HOME STATE MEMORIAL
                           Bouthillier St.
This is the home that the citizens of Galena
presented to General U. S. Grant on August   18,
1865, when he returned from the Civil War. Now a
State Memorial; admission free.

GENERAL GRANT DANCED AT THE DESOTO HOUSE

An Illinois Central "Special" - on September 11, 1865 - brought some forty military and civilian dignitaries from Chicago to attend the Complimentary Ball and Banquet honoring General U. S. Grant.

Five hundred invitations were extended for the great occasion. *Major General John A. Logan* spoke from the DeSoto House balcony, sustaining his reputation as an orator!

The great dining hall of the DeSoto House was superbly decorated. Flags of every description were festooned upon the pillars, and portraits of Grant and Logan and other generals adorned the walls. Muskets were stacked around the hall; and a huge American Eagle in bronze perched on a pedestal. The banquet table was lavishly and elegantly spread.

The assembled military personnel included *Major General Mason Brayman, Col. Orville E. Babcock, Col. Adam Badeau, Majors J. R. Hotalling, J. B. Dent, and S. Wait. Governor Richard J. Oglesby, Secretary of State O. M. Hatch, and State Treasurer Sharon Tyndale* were among the dignitaries. The press was represented by *Sam J. Medill* of the Chicago Tribune, and by reporters of more than a half dozen other newspapers.

General Grant tripped the light fantastic with the guests, then at 1:00 a. m. he with his family and staff withdrew, while the rest of the party kept on with the dance until 3:00 a.m.

On the following morning *General Grant* and his party left for Springfield, Illinois and St. Louis, Missouri in the four magnificent coaches which the Illinois Central Railroad furnished.

ELECTION NIGHT REMINISCENCE

Huge bonfires were lit on the hills, and residences were illuminated throughout the town. General Smith commanded the Galena Tanners, and Colonel Miller commanded the mounted artillery unit. The Galena Leadmine Band and the Dubuque Germania Band supplied the beat for the marching feet.

Several thousands marched in the torchlight parade to the Bouthillier Street residence of Ulysses S. Grant. Enroute, a large unoccupied building had been set afire, and as the procession passed this structure every timber blazed and the flames lighted up the area.

Three rousing cheers greeted the President-elect, and he made a brief speech from the piazza. The bands serenaded the future 18th President of the United States, and a magnificent display of fireworks was set off on the Grant home lawn. Within seconds after the signal Roman Candle was touched off, more than a thousand candles sent balls of fire into the air, shedding a brilliant light that illuminated the sky.

Then the paraders moved on to the residence of Hon. E. B. Washburne, who had just been elected to Congress for his 9th term. Cheered by the crowd, and serenaded by the bands, he responded with a brief and eloquent speech.

A similiar ceremony was held at the home of Major General John E. Smith, then the torchlight paraders wound their way around town before disbanding.

GALENA AND THE DESOTO HOUSE
HAVE SHARED IN THE PAGEANT OF HISTORY

Opened in April 1855 the 5 story, 240 room DeSoto House was "the most luxurious hotel in the west."

Ulysses S. Grant maintained his 1868 presidential campaign headquarters at the DeSoto House

On August 24, 1858 at 2 p.m Stephen A. Douglass, "The Little Giant," addressed a mass meeting from this same balcony

Abraham Lincoln spoke from the (now removed) balcony July 23, 1856. His closing sentence was later to become a civil war slogan "All this talk about the dissolution of the Union is humbug—nothing but folly. We WON'T dissolve the Union, and you SHAN'T "

By 1880 Galena's prosperity had faded, population and commerce declined, and the two upper stories (closed since 1875) were removed.
The original roof was raised on screw jacks, then lowered gradually as the two stories were removed

* * *

Of her it is said with no idle boast,
To men of great fame, she acted as host;
With pride she can point to her chambers today,
Where heroes renowned have once "hit the hay."
Reprinted from "Rhythm of the River"
with permission of author

Ceremonies April 30, 1960, unveiling the Illinois State Historical Society marker at the DeSoto House At this 6th Annual U S Grant Pilgrimage 1703 Boy Scouts took part in the ceremonies   Dubuque Telegraph Herald Photo

Way Back When... De Soto House Menu

BILL OF FARE
GALENA SUNDAY APRIL 29TH 1855

SOUP
MACARONI SOUP

FISH
BOILED BASS   BAKED SALMON

BOILED
HAM   CORNED BEEF
CHICKEN   LEG MUTTON
TONGUE

COLD
HAM   CORNED BEEF

ENTREES
KIDNEY AND PORK   PORK AND GREENS
MUTTON CURRY   BAKED PORK AND

ROAST
BEEF   MUTTON
PORK   PIG
LAMB-MINT SAUCE   TURKEY

VEGETABLES
BOILED POTATOES   TURNIPS
MASHED POTATOES   PARSNIP
ASPARAGUS   ONIONS

PASTRY and PUDDING
GRAPE PIE   APPLE PIE
GREEN PEACH PIE   GAGE PLUM PIE

DESSERT
NUTS   ICE CREAM   RAISINS

IN 1855 A ROOM AT THE De Soto HOUSE WAS PRICED TO INCLUDE FOUR MEALS A DAY. "BREAKFAST 6½ TO 9 O'CLOCK; DINNER 1½ O'CLOCK; TEA 6½ O'CLOCK; SUPPER 8 TO 9 O'CLOCK." RATE? $2°° DAILY PER PERSON.

A WINE LIST SHOWS CHAMPAGNE SOLD AT $2°° A QUART & $1°° A PINT, THAT MADEIRO SOLD FOR $2°° A QUART, & "BROWN STOUT LONDON PORTER" LIKEWISE ALE, AT 75¢ A QUART.

Today — OLD FASHIONED HOSPITALITY WITH MODERN ACCOMMODATIONS

De Soto House
230 SOUTH MAIN ST.   GALENA ILLINOIS
IN THE TOWN THAT TIME FORGOT

THE JO DAVIESS GUARD WAS DRILLED BY U. S. GRANT!

William Scheerer.   George Beebe.   George Salzer.   Ignatz Klein.   Anton Bahwell.   Charles Seitzberg.

Prof. G. A. Godat.   Samuel Starr.   Herman Ulverer.   Gen. A. L. Chetlain.   George S. Avery.   J. R. Lamb.

Five thousand persons gathered on the 25th of April 1861 to bid the 106-man JO DAVIESS GUARD "God Speed" when it departed from Galena for the battlefields of the Civil War.

Augustus L. Chetlain was the first man to sign the Muster Roll, closely followed by Wallace Campbell, J. Bates Dickson, and others. At Captain U. S. Grant's suggestion Augustus Chetlain was elected Captain of the Company. Wallace Campbell was elected First Lieutenant, and J. Bates Dickson was elected Second Lieutenant.

Patriotic women called upon Grant for advice regarding the correct regulation infantry uniform, then they solicited funds, bought material, commissioned tailors to cut the garments, and the women sewed the uniforms. Meanwhile Grant drilled these men, and within a few days the company was uniformed and ready to report at Springfield for assignment.

As departure hour arrived, the volunteers marched to the depot along streets lined with cheering well-wishers. They were led by the Galena Brass Band, and followed by Liberty Fire Company No. 1. They were flanked on the right by Neptune Fire Company No. 2, and on the left by Relief Hook & Ladder Co. No. 4. Members of Galena Fire Company No. 3 were next in the procession, just ahead of the Schreiners Brass Band, who was followed by the German Societies, Mayor, City Council, representatives of civic organizations and citizens.

In front of the DeSoto House the procession halted for brief ceremonies, at which a silk flag made by Galena ladies was presented to the Company. Mr. E. A. Small made the presentation and Captain Augustus L. Chetlain gave the acceptance speech. Captain U. S. Grant fell in at the rear left of the Company and marched with it across the Green Street Bridge to the Illinois Central Railroad Depot. Here brief addresses were given by Mayor Robert Brand and Rev. J. H. Vincent, and a revolver of rare workmanship was presented to Professor G. A. Godat, the color bearer.

Of the sixty companies accepted by the State of Illinois, the Jo Daviess Guard was the only one to arrive in Camp Yates fully uniformed, and with military precision and discipline. The Jo Daviess Guard became Company F of the Twelfth Regiment, Illinois Infantry, assigned to the right center of the Regiment and designated as the "Color Company".

GALENA WOMAN WAS A PRIVATE IN THE UNION ARMY

Galena-born Clarissa Emily Gear Hobbs served with the boys in blue, travelling with her husband, Dr. J. C. H. Hobbs, M D. In her Memoirs Mrs. Hobbs wrote. "The only way I could go with my husband was to have my name placed on the roster as a private soldier and detailed to work in the hospital. It was Col. Wood, a West Point man, who arranged the details; 'You can draw your rations as a soldier of the Iowa 12th, have two blankets issued to you, and can go that way' ".

Their first winter with troops was spent at the Regimental Hospital at St. Louis. In early January they were shipped to Smithland, Kentucky. Within a few hours after Northern Troops took Ft. Henry, the "Long Roll" sounded at Smithland. Soldiers left their sick beds to answer the call "to arms", rushing on to the transports waiting to carry them on to Fort Donelson on the Tennessee River.

All night the hospital staff heard guns booming, and the next morning news came that Fort Donelson was captured by Union forces. Soon the transports returned to Smithland, flags at half-mast, filled with wounded soldiers.

Mrs. Hobbs was recognized as a Nurse of the Iowa 12th, but at that time no provision had been made for nurses, and she wrote in her memoirs, "So I never got my $13.00 per month." She later received a government pension of $12.00 monthly.

Source "Autobiography of Clarissa E Gear Hobbs," Vol 17 Journal of the Illinois State Historical Society.

✦✦✦✦✦✦✦✦✦✦✦✦✦✦✦✦✦✦✦✦✦

YOUTH ANSWERED LINCOLN'S CALL!

THOMAS E. REYNOLDS of Galena, enlisted July 30, 1862, mustered in Sept. 4, 1862; mustered out June 10, 1865. He served with the Ninety-sixth Infantry-Co. I.

He enlisted as a Private at the age of 17, but was detailed as Drummer, and served with the Regimental Band till the close of the war; was never absent except for about three weeks in the spring of 1863; was present and acted with the Ambulance Corps in every engagement in which the Regiment participated.

His post-war activity was as a member of the firm of Fiddick & Reynolds, Boot and Shoe Dealers, Galena, Illinois.

Chicago Historical Society Reference Report, from History of the Ninety-Sixth Regiment, Illinois Volunteer Infantry Edited by Charles A Partridge Brown, Pettibone & Co., Chicago 1887 pb882. Also, Report of the Adjutant General of the State of Illinois Vol V p 457

FLAG OF THE GALENA LEAD MINE REGIMENT

Can be seen at the *Galena Historical Museum*. This was the first flag to enter Vicksburg when the city fell, July 4, 1863. The flag was brought to Galena by General Smith; and loaned to the Museum by his grandson, W. K. K. Smith.

THESE CIVIL WAR MILITARY LEADERS
LEFT GALENA TO SERVE AND SAVE THE UNION

Augustus L. Chetlain

John O. Duer

Jasper E. Maltby

Ely S Parker

John A. Rawlins

ULYSSES S. GRANT

William R. Rowley

John Carson Smith

John E Smith

Ilustrations. Courtesy Illinois State Historical Library—U S Grant, Ely S Parker, John A. Rawlins, William R Rowley and A. L Chetlain
Courtesy Chicago Historical Society—J A Maltby, John O Duer, J. E Smith and J. C. Smith

THE HERO'S WELCOME

"HAIL TO THE CHIEF WHO IN TRIUMPH ADVANCES."

Grand triumphal arch across Main Street, welcoming General U. S. Grant home,—on the 18th day of August 1865. The five-story DeSoto House, shown above, was a beehive of activity.

Grant and his party arrived in Galena on a 3 p. m. Illinois Central "special" train. Twenty-five thousand persons welcomed him amid the firing of cannon, and waving of flags. Carriages conveyed the General and his party from the depot to the DeSoto House, where ceremonies were held. The procession kept time to the music of the 15th Corps, the Germania, Dubuque and other bands.

The triumphal arch was trimmed with evergreens, "emblematic of the never fading honors that will encircle the brows of those that won them". A finely carved American Eagle, with the emblems of victory and peace in its beak, was mounted on the arch overlooking the grandstand and crowd in the street below.

On this arch stood thirty six young ladies dressed in white, each waving a national flag. As the General and Mrs. Grant approached they showered flowers along their pathway. The Hon. E. B. Washburne gave the welcoming address, and Rev. Vincent replied on behalf of Ulysses S. Grant.

At the close of the ceremonies Grant received the key to the home on the East side of the Galena River,—which is now known as the GRANT HOME STATE MEMORIAL. Taking up residence in his new home, he was once again "Grant— Our Citizen".

GRANT'S HOME LIFE DURING ELECTION WEEK

While a nation waited for the decisive election day, "Leslie Illustrated" sent a photographer to record the activities of Ulysses S Grant in his home town —Frank Leslie's Illustrated Newspaper Nov 14, 1868

A FAMILIAR SCENE in Galena even during election week Grant's daily schedule remained unchanged After lunch he rested or walked or went for a carriage drive

PRESIDENT ELECT U. S GRANT maintained his 1868 election campaign Headquarters at the DESOTO HOUSE Here he is shown chatting with the desk clerk.

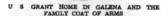

This is the 1857 home which the local citizens presented to Grant August 18, 1865, when he returned to Galena—the foremost military figure of his century
It is now the U S GRANT HOME, a state memorial

U S GRANT HOME IN GALENA AND THE FAMILY COAT OF ARMS

DEAR TO GRANT'S HEART was the twighlight hours when family and friends gathered at THE FIRESIDE CIRCLE

ULYSSES S. GRANT
18th President of the United States
1869 - 1877

"If the people want me, they'll elect me", Grant said. While his opponent stumped vigorously, General U. S. Grant remained in Galena, quiet and unassuming as always. The president-elect maintained personal headquarters at the De-Soto House. A Republican nominee, he was inevitable choice for President.

HISTORIANS HAVE RECORDED:

HIS PRIMARY CONCERN was for the public debt, and during his two administrations the national debt and taxes were reduced.

HE WAS THE FIRST PRESIDENT to propose a Civil Service based on merit; this much needed reform was finally accepted in 1883.

IN 1871 HE SECURED RATIFICATION of the Treaty of Washington, and the United States and Great Britain were the first countries to set an example to the world of "settlement by arbitration".

OTHER ACCOMPLISHMENTS OF HIS ADMINISTRATION included (a) an Indian Commission to improve the lot of the Indians; (b) establishment of Yellowstone National Park; (c) the study of water resources and problems of a watershed in California; (d) his efforts in behalf of better educational facilities; (e) his partially successful efforts to establish a merchant marine; (f) the enunciation of a tariff policy; and (g) provision for an orderly and peaceful succession after a contested presidential election.

HIS VISION WENT BEYOND HIS GENERATION, and many of the measures he favored were not adopted until after his administration ended.

Some of these were (a) the establishment of a naval base; (b) a market for the mutual exchange of trade with the Carribbean; (c) construction of an isthmian canal; (d) an organization for the settlement of international disputes, and many others.

Though the nation paid him homage as a General and as a President, and notwithstanding that kings had doffed their crowns to him, when ex-president U. S. Grant returned to his Galena home following two presidential terms and a trip around the world, he again resumed his place as "GRANT—OUR CITIZEN".

Source Military Affairs, Vol XVLL 1953

ULYSSES S. GRANT

A GALENA CHRONOLOGY

1860 — He moved to Galena, arriving aboard the streamer "Itasca", accompanied by his wife and their four small children.
His pre-war residence was a modest brick home at 121 High Street.

1861 — Captain U. S. Grant, answered President Abraham Lincoln's call for volunteers to save the Union.

Aug. 18, 1865 — Galena's greatest day - when 25,000 persons welcomed General Ulysses Grant home from the Civil War.

1868 — Ulysses S. Grant maintained his presidential campaign headquarters at the DeSoto House.

1869-1877 — Ulysses S. Grant - 18th President of the United States.

1879 — Following his two-year world tour Ex-President Grant returned to Galena, and was a familiar figure here, until

1881 — When he moved to New York. Expecting to return to Galena in his reclining years, he retained his home here.

BORN: April 27, 1822, at Point Pleasant, Ohio.

DIED: July 23, 1885, at McGregor, New York.

BURIED: In Grant's Tomb, Riverside, New York.

Chiseled on the sides of the stately granite shaft in Grant City Park, are the names of 424 heroes of Jo Daviess County who made the supreme sacrifice to preserve the Union.

THE FIRST ALL-YOUTH PROGRAM
IN THE NATION'S CIVIL WAR OBSERVANCE
took place in Galena April 29, 1961

Gen. Grant III Dines in Grant Memorial Home

An elegant 19th century party in the kerosene-lamp lighted home of his famous grandfather, arranged by the Department of Conservation, State of Illinois April 29, 1961.

A Record Shattering U. S. Grant Pilgrimage

Some of the 3,005 Boy Scouts, Explorers and Scouters from four states who took part in the ceremonies sponsored by the U S Grant Council, B S A, and the Galena Woman's Club. Gen U S Grant III, Chairman, National Civil War Centennial Commission and Dr Frank F Gross, Central Commander John T Graves, Camp No 516, Sons of Confederate Veterans, addressed the assembled scouts   —Galena Gazette Photos.

ANNUAL GRANT FETE   Boy Scout Pilgrimage, last Saturday in April. Girl Scout Day, first Saturday in May   Write Grant Birthday Committee, DeSoto House, Galena, Illinois

PILGRIMAGE THRU HISTORIC GALENA HOMES, sponsored by the Guild of the First Presbyterian Church, annually on the last weekend in September. Write Tour of Historic Homes, Galena, Illinois

Added attractions on Tour Weekend :

MARKET DAYS held on Market Square   Contact Jo Daviess County Home Bureau, Elizabeth, Ill.

ART EXHIBIT in the Market House.

VIOLET SHOW at Community Hall; write Ladies. Aid, Westminster United Presbyterian Church, Galena, Ill.

THE SWEET SHOPPE. Write Sigma Pi Sorority, Westminster United Presbyterian Church, Galena, Ill.

THE BLACKSMITH SHOP: Write Williard Richardson, Galena, Ill.

OLD FASHIONED MELODRAMA:

AVENUE OF ANTIQUES: Main Street merchants' windows display antiques, historic documents and items "out of the past".

THE CIVIL WAR CENTENNIAL

WILL AWAKEN RENEWED INTEREST IN GALENA, THE MOST

PERFECTLY PRESERVED HISTORIC TOWN IN ILLINOIS

THE U. S. GRANT PILGRIMAGE FOR BOY SCOUTS & EXPLORERS will stress a Civil War Centennial Commemoration theme in the Pilgrimages held on the last Saturday in April, 1961 thru 1965. Advance reservations required. Individual and unit awards For details write U. S. Grant Council, Boy Scouts of America, 616 W. Stephenson Street, Freeport Illinois.

CIVIL WAR CENTENNIAL COMMEMORATIONS
Plan to be with us!
U. S. GRANT PILGRIMAGE
FOR BOY SCOUTS AND EXPLORERS
7th Annual—Sat., April 29, 1961
8th Annual—Sat , April 28, 1962
9th Annual—Sat , April 27, 1963
10th Annual—Sat., April 25, 1964
11th Annual—Sat , April 24, 1965

July 2 thru 8, 1961, A City-wide Civil War Centennial Commemoration, with numerous special events and attractions. Historical pageant nightly July 4th thru 8th. Contact Galena Historical Society.

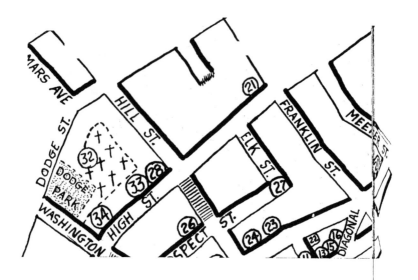

POINTS OF INTEREST

POINTS OF INTEREST

Black Hawk War Boulder 27 A-2
Bridge — pedestrian 18 B-4
Bridge — U. S. 20 .... A E-2
Cemetery — 1812 .... 32 A-1
Cobblestone Street 11 B-3
Commission House .... O C-2
County Court House - site 14 B-3
County Courthouse 20 A-3
De Soto House 1 C-2
Dowling House 23 B-2
Dowling Stone Store 15 B-3
Farrar, Amos — Cabin 12 B-3
Fell's Folly 40 B-2
Fire House No. 1 .... 44 C-2
Fire Station 25 B-2
Flood Gates .... D C-2
Flood Dike Protection 6 C-2
Frink-Walker Stage Site 4 C-2
Gazette & Advertiser 3 C-2
General Store 2 C-2
Grain Houses .... F C-2
Grant Memorial Home 63 D-4
Grant's Pre-war Home 33 B-1
Grant Park 58 D-3
Grant Statue 59 D-3
Grant, J. R. Store — site 7 C-2
Grant Store — reconstructed 5 C-2
Hotel DeSoto 1 C-2
Ill. Central R. R. Station 57 E-3
Kittoe, Edw. home 28 A-2
Levee .... B D-1
Library 52 D-1
Louisville House .... C C-2
Market House 9 B-3
Market Square 10 B-3
Methodist Manse (1st) 39 D-1
Mineral Museum - Spring St. near 54 D-1
Museum 45 C-2
Newhall Home 46 C-2
Old Town 17 A-4
Parochial School 50 B-1
Parochial School 21 A-3
Post Office 2 C-2
Post Office - 1st site 13 B-3
Quality Hill 38 B-2
Rawlins, J. A., home 29 A-1
Rowley, Wm. R., home 30 A-1
Smith, John E., home 55 E-1
Smith, Capt. O., home 60 D-4
Stahl, Fred, home 53 D-1
Steps — (Hill St. 26 B-2
        (School 37 C-1
        (Washington St. 43 C-2
Swimming Pool 19 A-4
Turner Hall 41 B-2
Union House 62 C-4
View .... (Scenic 59 C-1
         (Old World 35 C-1
Washburne, E. B. home 56 E-3

EAST SIDE —
Park Avenue and Bouthiller Street
See The Old Town Hall and Water
Filtration Plant

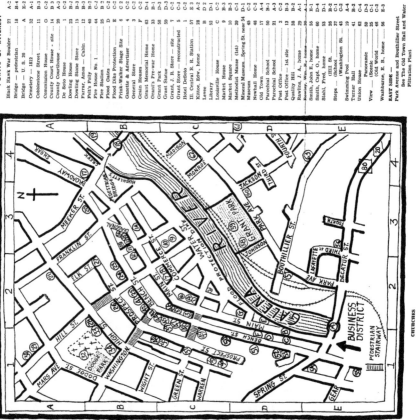

CHURCHES

State Memorial
OLD MARKET HOUSE
Inside can be seen "a graphic
exhibit of Illinois architecture"

CPSIA information can be obtained
at www.ICGtesting.com
Printed in the USA
BVHW09s2233230818
525365BV00019B/147/P

9 780483 088115